WEEKLY MEAL PLANNER
WITH GROCERY LIST

THIS MEAL PLANNER BELONGS TO:

_____

WEEKLY MEAL PLANNER

WEEK

	BREAKFAST	LUNCH	DINNER
MON			
TUES			
WED			
THURS			
FRI			
SAT			
SUN			

GROCERY LIST

WEEK

PRODUCE

MEAT & FISH

DAIRY

PANTRY

SNACKS

FROZEN

NOTES

WEEKLY MEAL PLANNER

WEEK

	BREAKFAST	LUNCH	DINNER
MON			
TUES			
WED			
THURS			
FRI			
SAT			
SUN			

GROCERY LIST

WEEK

PRODUCE

MEAT & FISH

DAIRY

PANTRY

SNACKS

FROZEN

NOTES

WEEKLY MEAL PLANNER

WEEK

	BREAKFAST	LUNCH	DINNER
MON			
TUES			
WED			
THURS			
FRI			
SAT			
SUN			

GROCERY LIST

PRODUCE

- ○
- ○
- ○
- ○
- ○
- ○
- ○
- ○
- ○
- ○
- ○
- ○
- ○
- ○
- ○
- ○
- ○
- ○
- ○

MEAT & FISH

- ○
- ○
- ○
- ○
- ○
- ○
- ○
- ○

DAIRY

- ○
- ○
- ○
- ○
- ○
- ○
- ○
- ○

PANTRY

- ○
- ○
- ○
- ○
- ○
- ○
- ○
- ○

SNACKS

- ○
- ○
- ○
- ○
- ○
- ○
- ○
- ○

FROZEN

- ○
- ○
- ○
- ○
- ○
- ○
- ○
- ○
- ○
- ○
- ○
- ○
- ○
- ○
- ○
- ○
- ○

NOTES

WEEKLY MEAL PLANNER

WEEK

	BREAKFAST	LUNCH	DINNER
MON			
TUES			
WED			
THURS			
FRI			
SAT			
SUN			

GROCERY LIST

WEEK

PRODUCE

MEAT & FISH

DAIRY

PANTRY

SNACKS

FROZEN

NOTES

WEEKLY MEAL PLANNER

WEEK

	BREAKFAST	LUNCH	DINNER
MON			
TUES			
WED			
THURS			
FRI			
SAT			
SUN			

GROCERY LIST

PRODUCE

MEAT & FISH

DAIRY

PANTRY

SNACKS

FROZEN

NOTES

WEEKLY MEAL PLANNER

	BREAKFAST	LUNCH	DINNER
MON			
TUES			
WED			
THURS			
FRI			
SAT			
SUN			

GROCERY LIST

WEEK

PRODUCE

- ◯
- ◯
- ◯
- ◯
- ◯
- ◯
- ◯
- ◯
- ◯
- ◯
- ◯
- ◯
- ◯
- ◯
- ◯
- ◯
- ◯

MEAT & FISH

- ◯
- ◯
- ◯
- ◯
- ◯
- ◯
- ◯
- ◯

DAIRY

- ◯
- ◯
- ◯
- ◯
- ◯
- ◯
- ◯
- ◯

PANTRY

- ◯
- ◯
- ◯
- ◯
- ◯
- ◯
- ◯
- ◯
- ◯

SNACKS

- ◯
- ◯
- ◯
- ◯
- ◯
- ◯
- ◯
- ◯

FROZEN

- ◯
- ◯
- ◯
- ◯
- ◯
- ◯
- ◯
- ◯
- ◯
- ◯
- ◯
- ◯
- ◯
- ◯
- ◯
- ◯
- ◯
- ◯

NOTES

WEEKLY MEAL PLANNER

WEEK

	BREAKFAST	LUNCH	DINNER
MON			
TUES			
WED			
THURS			
FRI			
SAT			
SUN			

GROCERY LIST

WEEK

PRODUCE

MEAT & FISH

DAIRY

PANTRY

SNACKS

FROZEN

NOTES

WEEKLY MEAL PLANNER

	WEEK

	BREAKFAST	LUNCH	DINNER
MON			
TUES			
WED			
THURS			
FRI			
SAT			
SUN			

GROCERY LIST

PRODUCE

MEAT & FISH

DAIRY

PANTRY

SNACKS

FROZEN

NOTES

WEEKLY MEAL PLANNER

WEEK

	BREAKFAST	LUNCH	DINNER
MON			
TUES			
WED			
THURS			
FRI			
SAT			
SUN			

GROCERY LIST

PRODUCE

○ _____
○ _____
○ _____
○ _____
○ _____
○ _____
○ _____
○ _____
○ _____
○ _____
○ _____
○ _____
○ _____
○ _____
○ _____
○ _____
○ _____

MEAT & FISH

○ _____
○ _____
○ _____
○ _____
○ _____
○ _____
○ _____
○ _____

DAIRY

○ _____
○ _____
○ _____
○ _____
○ _____
○ _____
○ _____
○ _____

PANTRY

○ _____
○ _____
○ _____
○ _____
○ _____
○ _____
○ _____
○ _____
○ _____
○ _____

SNACKS

○ _____
○ _____
○ _____
○ _____
○ _____
○ _____
○ _____
○ _____

FROZEN

○ _____
○ _____
○ _____
○ _____
○ _____
○ _____
○ _____
○ _____
○ _____
○ _____
○ _____
○ _____
○ _____
○ _____

NOTES

_____
_____
_____
_____
_____
_____
_____
_____
_____
_____
_____
_____
_____

WEEKLY MEAL PLANNER

WEEK

	BREAKFAST	LUNCH	DINNER
MON			
TUES			
WED			
THURS			
FRI			
SAT			
SUN			

GROCERY LIST

WEEK

PRODUCE

MEAT & FISH

DAIRY

PANTRY

SNACKS

FROZEN

NOTES

WEEKLY MEAL PLANNER

WEEK

	BREAKFAST	LUNCH	DINNER
MON			
TUES			
WED			
THURS			
FRI			
SAT			
SUN			

GROCERY LIST

PRODUCE

MEAT & FISH

DAIRY

PANTRY

SNACKS

FROZEN

NOTES

WEEKLY MEAL PLANNER

WEEK

	BREAKFAST	LUNCH	DINNER
MON			
TUES			
WED			
THURS			
FRI			
SAT			
SUN			

GROCERY LIST

WEEK

PRODUCE

MEAT & FISH

DAIRY

PANTRY

SNACKS

FROZEN

NOTES

WEEKLY MEAL
PLANNER

WEEK

	BREAKFAST	LUNCH	DINNER
MON			
TUES			
WED			
THURS			
FRI			
SAT			
SUN			

GROCERY LIST

PRODUCE

MEAT & FISH

DAIRY

PANTRY

SNACKS

FROZEN

NOTES

WEEKLY MEAL PLANNER

WEEK

	BREAKFAST	LUNCH	DINNER
MON			
TUES			
WED			
THURS			
FRI			
SAT			
SUN			

GROCERY LIST

WEEK

PRODUCE

MEAT & FISH

DAIRY

PANTRY

SNACKS

FROZEN

NOTES

WEEKLY MEAL PLANNER

WEEK

	BREAKFAST	LUNCH	DINNER
MON			
TUES			
WED			
THURS			
FRI			
SAT			
SUN			

GROCERY LIST

PRODUCE

MEAT & FISH

DAIRY

PANTRY

SNACKS

FROZEN

NOTES

WEEKLY MEAL PLANNER

WEEK

	BREAKFAST	LUNCH	DINNER
MON			
TUES			
WED			
THURS			
FRI			
SAT			
SUN			

GROCERY LIST

PRODUCE

MEAT & FISH

DAIRY

PANTRY

SNACKS

FROZEN

NOTES

WEEKLY MEAL PLANNER

WEEK

	BREAKFAST	LUNCH	DINNER
MON			
TUES			
WED			
THURS			
FRI			
SAT			
SUN			

GROCERY LIST

WEEK

PRODUCE

MEAT & FISH

DAIRY

PANTRY

SNACKS

FROZEN

NOTES

WEEKLY MEAL PLANNER

WEEK

	BREAKFAST	LUNCH	DINNER
MON			
TUES			
WED			
THURS			
FRI			
SAT			
SUN			

GROCERY LIST

WEEK

PRODUCE

- ○
- ○
- ○
- ○
- ○
- ○
- ○
- ○
- ○
- ○
- ○
- ○
- ○
- ○
- ○
- ○
- ○

MEAT & FISH

- ○
- ○
- ○
- ○
- ○
- ○
- ○

DAIRY

- ○
- ○
- ○
- ○
- ○
- ○
- ○

PANTRY

- ○
- ○
- ○
- ○
- ○
- ○
- ○
- ○

SNACKS

- ○
- ○
- ○
- ○
- ○
- ○
- ○

FROZEN

- ○
- ○
- ○
- ○
- ○
- ○
- ○
- ○
- ○
- ○
- ○
- ○
- ○
- ○
- ○

NOTES

WEEKLY MEAL PLANNER

WEEK

	BREAKFAST	LUNCH	DINNER
MON			
TUES			
WED			
THURS			
FRI			
SAT			
SUN			

GROCERY LIST

PRODUCE

MEAT & FISH

DAIRY

PANTRY

SNACKS

FROZEN

NOTES

WEEKLY MEAL PLANNER

WEEK

	BREAKFAST	LUNCH	DINNER
MON			
TUES			
WED			
THURS			
FRI			
SAT			
SUN			

GROCERY LIST

WEEK

PRODUCE

MEAT & FISH

DAIRY

PANTRY

SNACKS

FROZEN

NOTES

WEEKLY MEAL PLANNER

	BREAKFAST	LUNCH	DINNER
MON			
TUES			
WED			
THURS			
FRI			
SAT			
SUN			

GROCERY LIST

WEEK

PRODUCE

MEAT & FISH

DAIRY

PANTRY

SNACKS

FROZEN

NOTES

WEEKLY MEAL PLANNER

WEEK

	BREAKFAST	LUNCH	DINNER
MON			
TUES			
WED			
THURS			
FRI			
SAT			
SUN			

GROCERY LIST

WEEK

PRODUCE

MEAT & FISH

DAIRY

FROZEN

PANTRY

SNACKS

NOTES

WEEKLY MEAL PLANNER

| | WEEK |

	BREAKFAST	LUNCH	DINNER
MON			
TUES			
WED			
THURS			
FRI			
SAT			
SUN			

GROCERY LIST

WEEK

PRODUCE

MEAT & FISH

DAIRY

PANTRY

SNACKS

FROZEN

NOTES

WEEKLY MEAL PLANNER

	BREAKFAST	LUNCH	DINNER
MON			
TUES			
WED			
THURS			
FRI			
SAT			
SUN			

GROCERY LIST

WEEK

PRODUCE

MEAT & FISH

DAIRY

PANTRY

SNACKS

FROZEN

NOTES

WEEKLY MEAL PLANNER

WEEK

	BREAKFAST	LUNCH	DINNER
MON			
TUES			
WED			
THURS			
FRI			
SAT			
SUN			

GROCERY LIST

WEEK

PRODUCE

MEAT & FISH

DAIRY

PANTRY

SNACKS

FROZEN

NOTES

WEEKLY MEAL PLANNER

WEEK

	BREAKFAST	LUNCH	DINNER
MON			
TUES			
WED			
THURS			
FRI			
SAT			
SUN			

GROCERY LIST

PRODUCE

MEAT & FISH

DAIRY

PANTRY

SNACKS

FROZEN

NOTES

WEEKLY MEAL PLANNER

WEEK

	BREAKFAST	LUNCH	DINNER
MON			
TUES			
WED			
THURS			
FRI			
SAT			
SUN			

GROCERY LIST

WEEK

PRODUCE

MEAT & FISH

DAIRY

PANTRY

SNACKS

FROZEN

NOTES

WEEKLY MEAL PLANNER

WEEK

	BREAKFAST	LUNCH	DINNER
MON			
TUES			
WED			
THURS			
FRI			
SAT			
SUN			

GROCERY LIST

WEEK

PRODUCE

MEAT & FISH

DAIRY

PANTRY

SNACKS

FROZEN

NOTES

WEEKLY MEAL PLANNER

WEEK

	BREAKFAST	LUNCH	DINNER
MON			
TUES			
WED			
THURS			
FRI			
SAT			
SUN			

GROCERY LIST

WEEK

PRODUCE

MEAT & FISH

DAIRY

PANTRY

SNACKS

FROZEN

NOTES

WEEKLY MEAL PLANNER

	BREAKFAST	LUNCH	DINNER
MON			
TUES			
WED			
THURS			
FRI			
SAT			
SUN			

GROCERY LIST

WEEK

PRODUCE

MEAT & FISH

DAIRY

PANTRY

SNACKS

FROZEN

NOTES

WEEKLY MEAL PLANNER

WEEK

	BREAKFAST	LUNCH	DINNER
MON			
TUES			
WED			
THURS			
FRI			
SAT			
SUN			

GROCERY LIST

WEEK

PRODUCE

MEAT & FISH

DAIRY

PANTRY

SNACKS

FROZEN

NOTES

WEEKLY MEAL PLANNER

WEEK

	BREAKFAST	LUNCH	DINNER
MON			
TUES			
WED			
THURS			
FRI			
SAT			
SUN			

GROCERY LIST

[WEEK]

PRODUCE

MEAT & FISH

DAIRY

PANTRY

SNACKS

FROZEN

NOTES

WEEKLY MEAL PLANNER

	WEEK

	BREAKFAST	LUNCH	DINNER
MON			
TUES			
WED			
THURS			
FRI			
SAT			
SUN			

GROCERY LIST

`[` WEEK `]`

PRODUCE

- ○
- ○
- ○
- ○
- ○
- ○
- ○
- ○
- ○
- ○
- ○
- ○
- ○
- ○
- ○
- ○
- ○

MEAT & FISH

- ○
- ○
- ○
- ○
- ○
- ○
- ○
- ○

DAIRY

- ○
- ○
- ○
- ○
- ○
- ○
- ○

PANTRY

- ○
- ○
- ○
- ○
- ○
- ○
- ○
- ○
- ○

SNACKS

- ○
- ○
- ○
- ○
- ○
- ○
- ○

FROZEN

- ○
- ○
- ○
- ○
- ○
- ○
- ○
- ○
- ○
- ○
- ○
- ○
- ○
- ○
- ○

NOTES

WEEKLY MEAL PLANNER

WEEK

	BREAKFAST	LUNCH	DINNER
MON			
TUES			
WED			
THURS			
FRI			
SAT			
SUN			

GROCERY LIST

PRODUCE

MEAT & FISH

DAIRY

PANTRY

SNACKS

FROZEN

NOTES

WEEKLY MEAL PLANNER

	WEEK

	BREAKFAST	LUNCH	DINNER
MON			
TUES			
WED			
THURS			
FRI			
SAT			
SUN			

GROCERY LIST

PRODUCE

MEAT & FISH

DAIRY

PANTRY

SNACKS

FROZEN

NOTES

WEEKLY MEAL PLANNER

WEEK

	BREAKFAST	LUNCH	DINNER
MON			
TUES			
WED			
THURS			
FRI			
SAT			
SUN			

GROCERY LIST

PRODUCE

MEAT & FISH

DAIRY

PANTRY

SNACKS

FROZEN

NOTES

WEEKLY MEAL PLANNER

WEEK

	BREAKFAST	LUNCH	DINNER
MON			
TUES			
WED			
THURS			
FRI			
SAT			
SUN			

GROCERY LIST

WEEK

PRODUCE

MEAT & FISH

DAIRY

PANTRY

SNACKS

FROZEN

NOTES

WEEKLY MEAL PLANNER

WEEK

	BREAKFAST	LUNCH	DINNER
MON			
TUES			
WED			
THURS			
FRI			
SAT			
SUN			

GROCERY LIST

WEEK

PRODUCE

MEAT & FISH

DAIRY

PANTRY

SNACKS

FROZEN

NOTES

WEEKLY MEAL PLANNER

	BREAKFAST	LUNCH	DINNER
MON			
TUES			
WED			
THURS			
FRI			
SAT			
SUN			

GROCERY LIST

WEEK

PRODUCE

MEAT & FISH

DAIRY

PANTRY

SNACKS

FROZEN

NOTES

WEEKLY MEAL PLANNER

WEEK

	BREAKFAST	LUNCH	DINNER
MON			
TUES			
WED			
THURS			
FRI			
SAT			
SUN			

GROCERY LIST

WEEK

PRODUCE

MEAT & FISH

DAIRY

PANTRY

SNACKS

FROZEN

NOTES

WEEKLY MEAL PLANNER

	BREAKFAST	LUNCH	DINNER
MON			
TUES			
WED			
THURS			
FRI			
SAT			
SUN			

GROCERY LIST

WEEK

PRODUCE

MEAT & FISH

DAIRY

PANTRY

SNACKS

FROZEN

NOTES

WEEKLY MEAL PLANNER

WEEK

	BREAKFAST	LUNCH	DINNER
MON			
TUES			
WED			
THURS			
FRI			
SAT			
SUN			

GROCERY LIST

WEEK

PRODUCE

MEAT & FISH

DAIRY

PANTRY

SNACKS

FROZEN

NOTES

WEEKLY MEAL PLANNER

	BREAKFAST	LUNCH	DINNER
MON			
TUES			
WED			
THURS			
FRI			
SAT			
SUN			

GROCERY LIST

WEEK

PRODUCE

MEAT & FISH

DAIRY

PANTRY

SNACKS

FROZEN

NOTES

WEEKLY MEAL PLANNER

	BREAKFAST	LUNCH	DINNER
MON			
TUES			
WED			
THURS			
FRI			
SAT			
SUN			

GROCERY LIST

WEEK

PRODUCE

MEAT & FISH

DAIRY

PANTRY

SNACKS

FROZEN

NOTES

WEEKLY MEAL PLANNER

WEEK

	BREAKFAST	LUNCH	DINNER
MON			
TUES			
WED			
THURS			
FRI			
SAT			
SUN			

GROCERY LIST

WEEK

PRODUCE

MEAT & FISH

DAIRY

PANTRY

SNACKS

FROZEN

NOTES

WEEKLY MEAL PLANNER

WEEK

	BREAKFAST	LUNCH	DINNER
MON			
TUES			
WED			
THURS			
FRI			
SAT			
SUN			

GROCERY LIST

PRODUCE

MEAT & FISH

DAIRY

PANTRY

SNACKS

FROZEN

NOTES

WEEKLY MEAL PLANNER

WEEK

	BREAKFAST	LUNCH	DINNER
MON			
TUES			
WED			
THURS			
FRI			
SAT			
SUN			

GROCERY LIST

WEEK

PRODUCE

MEAT & FISH

DAIRY

PANTRY

SNACKS

FROZEN

NOTES

WEEKLY MEAL PLANNER

WEEK

	BREAKFAST	LUNCH	DINNER
MON			
TUES			
WED			
THURS			
FRI			
SAT			
SUN			

GROCERY LIST

WEEK

PRODUCE

- ◯ _____
- ◯ _____
- ◯ _____
- ◯ _____
- ◯ _____
- ◯ _____
- ◯ _____
- ◯ _____
- ◯ _____
- ◯ _____
- ◯ _____
- ◯ _____
- ◯ _____
- ◯ _____

MEAT & FISH

- ◯ _____
- ◯ _____
- ◯ _____
- ◯ _____
- ◯ _____
- ◯ _____
- ◯ _____

DAIRY

- ◯ _____
- ◯ _____
- ◯ _____
- ◯ _____
- ◯ _____
- ◯ _____
- ◯ _____

PANTRY

- ◯ _____
- ◯ _____
- ◯ _____
- ◯ _____
- ◯ _____
- ◯ _____
- ◯ _____

SNACKS

- ◯ _____
- ◯ _____
- ◯ _____
- ◯ _____
- ◯ _____
- ◯ _____

FROZEN

- ◯ _____
- ◯ _____
- ◯ _____
- ◯ _____
- ◯ _____
- ◯ _____
- ◯ _____
- ◯ _____
- ◯ _____
- ◯ _____
- ◯ _____
- ◯ _____
- ◯ _____

NOTES

_____
_____
_____
_____
_____
_____
_____
_____
_____
_____
_____
_____

WEEKLY MEAL PLANNER

WEEK

	BREAKFAST	LUNCH	DINNER
MON			
TUES			
WED			
THURS			
FRI			
SAT			
SUN			

GROCERY LIST

PRODUCE

MEAT & FISH

DAIRY

PANTRY

SNACKS

FROZEN

NOTES

WEEKLY MEAL PLANNER

	BREAKFAST	LUNCH	DINNER
MON			
TUES			
WED			
THURS			
FRI			
SAT			
SUN			

GROCERY LIST

WEEK

PRODUCE

MEAT & FISH

DAIRY

PANTRY

SNACKS

FROZEN

NOTES

WEEKLY MEAL PLANNER

	BREAKFAST	LUNCH	DINNER
MON			
TUES			
WED			
THURS			
FRI			
SAT			
SUN			

GROCERY LIST

WEEK

PRODUCE

MEAT & FISH

DAIRY

PANTRY

SNACKS

FROZEN

NOTES

WEEKLY MEAL PLANNER

WEEK

	BREAKFAST	LUNCH	DINNER
MON			
TUES			
WED			
THURS			
FRI			
SAT			
SUN			

GROCERY LIST

PRODUCE

MEAT & FISH

DAIRY

PANTRY

SNACKS

FROZEN

NOTES

DATE _____

DATE _____

DATE

Printed in Great Britain
by Amazon